Cyrano and The Nose

Based on *Cyrano de Bergerac* by Edmund Rostand and *The Nose* by Nikolai Gogol

Michael Leviton

SCHOLASTIC INC.
New York Toronto London Auckland Sydney
Mexico City New Delhi Hong Kong Buenos Aires

**Illustrations
Erin + Kelly Carty**

Text copyright © 2004 by Scholastic Inc.
Illustrations copyright © 2004 by Erin and Kelly Carty.
All rights reserved. Published by Scholastic Inc.
Printed in the U.S.A.

ISBN 0-439-68249-5

SCHOLASTIC, READ 180, and associated logos and designs are trademarks and/or registered trademarks of Scholastic Inc.

LEXILE is a registered trademark of MetaMetrics, Inc.

6 7 8 9 10   23   12 11 10

Contents

Cyrano has a big nose. And a big nose can really get in the way!

1

Cyrano

Cyrano de Bergerac had the biggest nose in all of France. When he walked down the street, strangers gasped and pointed. But Cyrano wasn't all nose. He also had a big brain. He was the **cleverest** man in France.

Cyrano was in love with a beautiful woman named Roxanne. Like Cyrano, Roxanne was very clever, and the two of

cleverest smartest

Cyrano was in love with Roxanne,
but he didn't dare tell her.

them had been friends for years. Cyrano had never dared to tell her how he felt. He didn't think any woman could love a man with such a big nose.

Finally, one day, Cyrano got up the nerve to write Roxanne a love letter. He had plans to see a play with her that night. He told himself that he would give her the letter if the right moment came.

A Battle of Wits

That night, when Cyrano saw Roxanne waiting outside the theater, he thought of a hundred **poetic** ways to describe her beauty. But all he said was, "Hello." She said hello back and they went inside.

The lights **dimmed**, and an actor walked onto the stage. Roxanne

---

poetic beautiful; said or done in a way that sounds like a poem

dimmed became less bright

"Roxanne, *everybody* hates the Count," Cyrano laughed.

whispered, "That's the Count! I didn't know he was in this play. I hate him!"

"Everybody hates the Count!" Cyrano laughed. "Do you have a special reason?"

Roxanne answered, "I hate him because he's in love with me—"

Cyrano interrupted, "You must hate

the whole world then."

Roxanne smiled. "You didn't let me finish," she said. "The Count is in love with me—and he's a creep. He **proposed** to me yesterday, and it took me an hour to wash off all the drool."

"He's a very powerful man in the army," Cyrano said. "When the Count doesn't like someone, he sends the poor man off to war!"

"I know! He expects everyone to take orders from him." Roxanne sighed. "I can't stand to look at him! Can we please get out of here?"

"I've got a better idea," Cyrano said. "We'll just put on a better show!"

Cyrano jumped onto the stage and said, "Count, get off the stage!"

---

proposed asked someone to marry them

The audience cheered. Nobody liked the Count, and everybody loved Cyrano.

"But I'm the star," the Count said.

"Count, if you're a star, you should be a million miles away! So scram! If you're a star, shoot out of here!" Cyrano said. The crowd laughed and **applauded**. Cyrano looked up at Roxanne and saw her smiling.

The Count's face had turned red. He pointed his finger at Cyrano, and shouted, "Oh yeah? Well, your nose is big!"

The crowd fell silent. Not a single laugh could be heard.

Cyrano just smiled and said, "Count, you've wasted such an **opportunity**! My nose is the best target for **insults** in all of France! And that's the cleverest thing you

---

applauded clapped for

opportunity a chance

insults mean comments about someone

"Sorry, Count," Cyrano said. "Your joke wasn't clever at all."

can say?" The crowd laughed again.

The Count's face got even redder. "At least I'm not an ugly big-nose!" he shouted. The crowd was silent again.

"Sorry, Count," Cyrano said. "'Big-nose' isn't clever either. Here, let me help." Cyrano tapped his nose with his finger to show he was thinking. "Well, Count, you could say, 'At least I don't have to pick my nose with a shovel!'" The audience laughed and applauded.

"Or," Cyrano went on, "You could say, 'Hey, Cyrano! Pinnochio called! He wants his nose back!'" The crowd screamed with laughter.

"Or Count, why not just call me, 'CyraNOSE de BOOGERac!'" The crowd could not stop laughing.

Finally, the Count could not stand the **humiliation**. He ran off the stage as fast as he could. Cyrano bowed, and the crowd threw roses.

Roxanne in Love

When Cyrano returned to Roxanne, she kissed his cheek. "That was perfect!" she said. "That's probably the first time anyone's ever insulted the Count! And you are so funny!" Then her face became very serious. "Cyrano," she said, moving closer to him. "I have something very important to tell you, something from deep in my heart that I want to **confess**."

"You do?" Cyrano said. He tried to think of how he could kiss Roxanne without his nose poking out her eye.

humiliation embarrassment
confess to admit something

"Cyrano, I have something very important to confess,"
Roxanne said.

"Cyrano," Roxanne said. "I'm in love. But the man I love is shy. I think he loves me, too, but he's too shy to tell me. If only he'd ask me to marry him, I'd be his wife!"

Cyrano thought to himself, *Roxanne doesn't care that I have a big nose! She wants **romance**, poetry, a man with wit! It's what I've*

romance something having to do with love

always dreamed of! She wants me!

Cyrano was ready to fall onto his knees to propose to Roxanne. But then she said, "Even though I've never spoken to this handsome man, I know our love will last forever."

Cyrano coughed. "You've never spoken to him?" He paused. "And he's handsome?!"

"Cyrano!" Roxanne said. "Your face is all red! What's wrong?"

"Nothing, nothing," Cyrano said. He was holding his nose in his hand. He often held his nose when he got upset. "Nothing's wrong. I'm just curious. Who is this man?"

"His name is Christian. He's new in town. And he's the only man I'll ever love.

Please, Cyrano, help me. Tell him to write me tomorrow!"

"Okay, Roxanne," Cyrano said sadly, bowing his head, his nose pointing at the floor.

Cyrano's Plan

The next day, Cyrano found Christian and stopped him on the street. Christian was a tall, **muscular**, handsome man. Cyrano said to him, "I'm Cyrano, a friend of Roxanne's. Do you know her?"

"Of course," Christian said. "She's the hottest woman in town!"

Cyrano said, "Well, she wants you to write her a letter tonight. She's in love with you."

"Oh, no!" Christian said. "Not again!"

---

muscular having a lot of muscles

"Does a beautiful woman fall in love with you every day?" Cyrano asked.

Christian put his head in his hands.

"*Not again?*" Cyrano replied. "Does a beautiful woman fall in love with you every day?"

"No! Women always *think* they're in love with me. They think I'm interesting just because I'm handsome. Then, when I talk to them, they think I'm dumb, and they laugh at me! I'm just not good with words!" Christian waved his hands in the air. "I'm supposed to write her a letter? What do I say?"

"Your problem is the opposite of mine," Cyrano said. "I am an ugly man, but I'm a clever poet. You are a handsome man with no words! Let's work as a team. I'll write and speak for you!"

"Why would you do that, Cyrano?"

"It's a **challenge**," Cyrano said.

"Hey, you can't fool me! I know what's going on here! I'm not that dumb!" Christian said, knocking on his head with his fist as if to show Cyrano it wasn't hollow. "Cyrano, you're in love with Roxanne yourself! That's why you want to write her love letters!"

Cyrano pretended to laugh and said,

challenge something that takes extra work or effort to do

"No, Christian, I've never been in love. I just imagine what love is like." He pulled his letter to Roxanne from his pocket. "I write love letters to **imaginary** women, women I will probably never meet. You might say I write love letters to my own dreams. But you should give them to Roxanne." He shook Christian's hand. "I will sign your name and send the letter immediately."

The Count's Revenge

The next day, Cyrano asked Roxanne what she thought of Christian's letter.

"It was so beautiful!" Roxanne said. "He loves me so much, and he says it so poetically. I have a date with him tonight."

"Oh," Cyrano said. "What will you two

---

imaginary made-up

Roxanne and Cyrano had no idea the Count was spying on them.

talk about?"

"We'll probably just whisper in the dark about love. I'll ask him how much he loves me. And he'll come up with all kinds of beautiful ways to tell me."

Cyrano ran to get Christian. But just as he left Roxanne, he saw the Count hiding behind a tree, spying on her! The Count's face was all red, and his teeth were **clenched** in anger! Cyrano knew the Count had heard everything!

Then, the Count turned around and saw Cyrano. He smiled wickedly. He waved at Cyrano and called, "Hey, big-nose! Come here! I have some important news that I'm sure will interest you! It's about Roxanne!"

Cyrano walked over to him.

"I just wanted to let you know that you're going off to war tomorrow," the Count said. "I signed the papers an hour ago. I'm sending every man in town to the front lines!"

The Count laughed. "While you and all the other men are marching right into enemy bullets, I'll be happy here with my

---

clenched held together tightly

new wife: Roxanne! I'll make her marry me, and then I'll have her all to myself!"

"Don't *count* on it, Count!" Cyrano said.

The Count replied, "Shut up, big-nose!"

"'Big-nose' is still not funny, Count. You blew it again," Cyrano said. "I've got the nose, but you're the one who blew it!"

Christian Speaks for Himself

Cyrano found Christian sitting in the park feeding the birds. "Christian," Cyrano said, "Roxanne wants to see you tonight. You need romantic things to tell her, so I have some lines for you to **memorize**."

"No, thanks," Christian said. "I'll be okay. I can speak for myself."

"What do you mean?" Cyrano asked.

memorize to learn something by heart

"I was just nervous before," Christian said. "Now that I know Roxanne loves me, I can just be myself."

"Okay," Cyrano said. "Well, I'll come along just in case."

So, Christian went to Roxanne's house and threw pebbles at her window. Cyrano hid in the shadows.

Roxanne came out onto the **balcony** in her nightgown. She looked beautiful in the moonlight. "Who is it out there in the dark?" she asked.

"It's me—Christian," he said. Then there was a long silence. Christian knew he was supposed to say something, but he didn't know what.

Then Roxanne asked, "Why aren't you saying anything?"

balcony a platform on the outside of a building

"What do you want me to say?" Christian said.

"Tell me how much you love me," Roxanne said.

"Ummm . . . I love you very, very much?"

"You're ruining everything!" Roxanne said. "The only reason I like you is because you're a poet! And you're definitely not being very poetic!"

"I'm not?" Christian said.

Roxanne ran inside her room and slammed the door.

"Cyrano, you must help me!" Christian said **desperately**. "I've really fallen in love with Roxanne! She really understands me! If I lose Roxanne, I don't know what I'll do! I'll die of sadness!"

desperately with a lot of need

"Roxanne, I'll always love you!"
Cyrano said, pretending to be Christian.

"Calm down," Cyrano said. "Throw some more pebbles at her window. I'll do the talking this time."

Christian threw more pebbles. Roxanne came out onto the balcony again and said, "Go away; you don't love me anymore."

Cyrano said, "To stop loving you would be like stopping the sun from rising!"

Roxanne heard so much love behind this voice that she nearly fainted. "Really?" she said.

"Of course, my love," Cyrano said. "Stopping my love would be like stopping a summer breeze."

Roxanne's heart beat faster. She said, "Your voice sounds so different than it did a minute ago!"

"It's just the night air and the moonlight," Cyrano went on, "and the **intensity** of my feelings."

This went on for an hour, Roxanne falling more and more in love with this voice and its beautiful words.

The Secret Wedding

Cyrano knew that he had to do more than make Roxanne *love* Christian. He had to get her to *marry* Christian before **dawn**! Otherwise, Roxanne would be left alone with the Count after Christian, Cyrano, and the other men were sent off to war!

Cyrano called up to Roxanne, "Though I am here with you, I feel like I'm alone. Until you are my wife, truly mine forever,

intensity strength
dawn the first light of morning

every moment will only bring sharp, painful loneliness."

"Well, let's marry tonight, in secret!" Roxanne shouted. "I'll get dressed and be right down."

She went inside and Christian said. "But Cyrano, are you sure you want me to marry her?"

"Of course!" Cyrano said.

"Are you sure you're not in love with her yourself?" Christian asked. "The way you sound when you talk to her, it sounds like you love her even more than I do."

Cyrano pretended to laugh. "A great speaker seems to be in love with everyone he talks to," Cyrano said. At that, Cyrano jumped back into the bushes. Roxanne came out in a beautiful dress, and she and

Christian ran off to find a priest. Before dawn, the happy couple was married.

Love and War

The next day, Cyrano and Christian were sent off to war. They spent the next year **dodging** enemy bullets. During that time, Cyrano secretly wrote Roxanne every day and signed each letter with Christian's name. Christian had no idea.

One day, Roxanne came to visit. Cyrano raced to Christian's room to tell him about the letters.

"Are you crazy?" Christian shouted. "You wrote her every day? And she's here now? How could you do this to me? What do I say?"

Just then, Roxanne knocked on the

dodging getting out of the way of something

door. Christian opened it, and Roxanne hugged him. She didn't notice that Cyrano was in the room.

"Christian, your letters drew me to you!" Roxanne said. "Your letters have showed me your soul! If a bomb went off and took your face, I would still love you just as much. Because I love you for your letters, not your face!"

"Oh, that's nice," said Christian. "Hold on, Roxanne. I need to tell Cyrano something." Christian pulled away from her and walked over to Cyrano. He whispered, "She loves *you*, not *me*! She says she loves my letters, my soul! That means *you*. I know you love her, too. Go to her and explain."

"I can't," said Cyrano sadly, touching

his nose.

"Yes, you can," Christian said. He grabbed Cyrano by the arm and pulled him to Roxanne. "Roxanne," he said, "Cyrano has something to tell you." Then, Christian left the two alone.

When Cyrano looked into Roxanne's eyes again, he knew he should tell her the truth. But just as he started to speak, he heard gunfire outside. They ran out the door and found Christian on the ground covered in blood. He had been shot!

Roxanne screamed. She and Cyrano ran to Christian. Roxanne could not stop crying. Cyrano whispered into his ear, "Christian, I told her the truth! But she says she still loves you!"

Christian looked up at Cyrano and

"Roxanne still loves you,"
Cyrano whispered to Christian.

smiled. Then he looked at Roxanne. She hugged him, and he died in her arms.

Cyrano knew now he could never tell Roxanne the truth. Instead, he pulled his latest letter from his pocket and said, "I found this in Christian's jacket."

Fifteen years passed. Roxanne never

got over Christian's death. She stopped leaving her house. She put black cloth over all the windows and stayed inside in the dark all day. Cyrano visited her every Saturday, but never told her the truth. He just sat in the dark with her and talked with her about Christian.

The Truth Comes Out

Then, one day the Count sent Cyrano a message. It said Cyrano was dead if he visited Roxanne again. The Count was still jealous of anyone who spent time with her!

But Cyrano would not stop visiting Roxanne. One day Cyrano knocked on her door, and one of the Count's servants dropped a brick on his head.

Roxanne opened the door. She said,

"Cyrano, your head is bleeding!"

"That's just an old wound reopened," Cyrano replied.

"Some wounds never heal at all," Roxanne said, putting her hand on her broken heart.

Cyrano came inside and pretended he wasn't in pain. But he knew he was about to die. He said, "Can I ask you a favor, Roxanne? I always wanted to read Christian's last letter. Could I read it now?"

She pulled the letter from her drawer and said, "Yes, you have my **permission**, but it's too dark in here to read it."

They sat on the sofa, and Cyrano started reading the letter out loud.

"You must have really good eyes. I don't know how you can read in this

permission the act of allowing something to happen

"Cyrano, why didn't you tell me you wrote the letters?"
Roxanne cried.

darkness," Roxanne said. But then she realized Cyrano was not reading—he was **reciting** the letter from memory! "Cyrano, now I see!" she said. "You wrote all those letters! And it was you at the balcony that night!"

"No, you're wrong," Cyrano said.

"You're lying!" Roxanne continued. "I know it was you, Cyrano! Why didn't you ever tell me? Is it because of your nose? A big nose cannot ruin a beautiful soul!"

And before Cyrano could say anything, before he could come up with either a **witty** remark or a poetic one, he died.

Roxanne put her arms around him and cried. She had only loved one man. But she had lost him twice.

reciting saying something that you have learned by heart

witty funny in a smart way

*Suddenly Kovalyev's nose has
a mind of its own!*

2

The Nose

When Kovalyev woke up, his first thought was about the pimple that had appeared on his nose the day before.

He walked to the bathroom to look at the pimple. But when he saw his reflection, he saw that the pimple wasn't there. This would have been great news, except that the rest of his nose had disappeared as well!

"What's happened?" Kovalyev shouted.

**Kovalyev looked in the mirror and saw that his
nose had disappeared!**

"I must see a doctor immediately!"

Kovalyev dressed and ran outside. As he ran down the street, he **occasionally** checked his reflection in store windows. He felt sure it was impossible to lose one's nose like this, but each mirror reflected the same smooth spot where his nose had once stood.

"How disgusting!" Kovalyev thought. "If only there was something in my nose's place! Even an ear in the middle of my face would be better than this!"

Just then, Kovalyev saw something that made him stop in his tracks! His nose! And the nose was not sitting **innocently** in the trash as one might expect! It was getting out of a taxi, dressed in a suit!

Kovalyev couldn't believe what he was

occasionally once in a while
innocently not doing anything wrong

**Kovalyev followed the nose and saw it
heading into a church!**

seeing. The day before, his nose could
neither ride nor walk! Today, it was out
on the street in an **expensive** suit!

Kovalyev followed the nose and saw it
heading into a church! "I didn't know my
nose was religious!" Kovalyev thought.

When Kovalyev made it inside the

expensive costing a lot of money

church, he saw that the Nose had found a seat.

"My nose really has a lot of nerve! He has no right to leave my face!" Kovalyev thought. "I should go tell him a thing or two! But how should I put it?" Kovalyev thought for a moment and still had no idea what to say. "Well, I'm sure something will come to me!" he decided. "I just need to talk to my nose man-to-man for a minute." Kovalyev paused. "Or would it be man-to-nose?"

Kovalyev walked up to the praying Nose. Up close, Kovalyev could see the Nose's huge, ugly pimple!

Kovalyev wanted to tap the Nose's shoulder, but the Nose had no shoulders. Then Kovalyev had a better idea to get the

Nose's attention! He decided to tap the Nose right on his pimple! That would show the Nose how mad he was.

When Kovalyev poked the pimple, the Nose turned around and glared at him. "What do you think you're doing, jerk?" the Nose asked. His voice came from his giant **nostril**, which opened and closed like a mouth!

Kovalyev suddenly became **timid**. "Oh . . . I'm really very sorry, sir," he said. "But I just thought . . . well, I wanted to ask . . . ummm . . ."

"Sir, you're making a scene!" the Nose said. "Everyone is staring."

Kovalyev saw that he and the Nose had become the center of attention. He tried to pull himself together. "Sir!" he said.

---

nostril one of the two openings in your nose through which you breathe and smell

timid shy

"You have no right to be here!"

"I can go wherever I like," said the Nose.

"Do you expect me to just walk around without a nose?!" Kovalyev asked.

"My dear sir," the Nose replied. "Please calm down."

Kovalyev was turning red with anger. He hated this rude nose. He began to shout, "You are my nose! Get back on my face immediately!" Kovalyev's voice echoed through the church.

The Nose said, "My dear sir, you are mistaken. We have never met. And I am not a nose." The Nose then paused to sneeze. Snot flew all over the floor. And all over Kovalyev!

Kovalyev pulled out his handkerchief to clean himself off. Then he turned and

"My dear sir," the Nose said. "I am not a nose. You are mistaken."

started walking out of the church. As he neared the door, a beautiful woman walked past him. Kovalyev stood up straight and smiled at her. She put her hand to her lovely mouth in horror!

This reminded Kovalyev that he had no nose. He watched as the woman took a seat next to the Nose. She whispered something to the Nose, and they laughed. She smiled and put her arm around him.

"I've heard that love is blind!" Kovalyev thought. "But this is crazy! Doesn't she care that he has a huge pimple?" Kovalyev was mad with jealousy!

In his rage, Kovalyev thought of a plan.

He ran to the newspaper office. "Excuse me, sir," Kovalyev told the man at the desk. "I'd like to buy an ad. Please write this down.

"My nose has escaped my face," Kovalyev told
the man behind the desk.

WANTED: MY NOSE. IT HAS ESCAPED
MY FACE. IT IS RUNNING AROUND
TOWN IN AN EXPENSIVE SUIT AND
FLIRTING WITH WOMEN! I WILL OFFER
A REWARD TO ANYONE WHO CAN
RETURN MY NOSE TO MY FACE."

But the man at the desk did not write

down anything Kovalyev said.

"You're not writing it down!" Kovalyev said. "Here, let me tell you again—"

"I cannot print your ad," said the man.

"Why not?" Kovalyev asked.

"Because it doesn't make sense. For example, how can a nose wear a suit?"

"You idiot! I don't have time to explain everything!" He stormed out of the office and walked home.

The Nose Gets Caught

When Kovalyev got home, a police **carriage** was waiting. An officer asked him, "Have you been looking for your nose?"

"Yes! Yes!" Kovalyev shouted. "Have you captured him?"

"You're lucky," the officer said. "Your

carriage a vehicle with wheels, often pulled by horses

"My nose is a scoundrel!" Kovalyev said.

nose almost got away. He had bought a train ticket to Paris. But then someone realized his **passport** was fake! When the police searched him, they found a million dollars worth of stolen gold coins in his nostril!"

"My nose is a **scoundrel**!" Kovalyev said. "Let me see him."

The Nose was sitting in the police

passport a booklet that says what country you're from. It is often necessary for travel.
scoundrel a bad person

officer's carriage. He said nothing as Kovalyev and the officer marched him inside. They sat him down on the couch and started to figure out how to reattach him to Kovalyev's face.

Note for the Reader

Yes, dear reader, I know this story seems unlikely. There are many parts that even I, your author, find hard to believe. But all the same, when you think about it, there is something important to learn from all this madness. Whatever anyone says, the world is stranger than you'd think. These things happen. They don't happen often, but they do happen sometimes. And they can even happen to you!

Glossary

applauded *(verb)* clapped for

balcony *(noun)* a platform on the outside of a building

carriage *(noun)* a vehicle with wheels, often pulled by horses

challenge *(noun)* something that takes extra work or effort to do

clenched *(adjective)* held together tightly *(related words: clench, clenching)*

cleverest *(adjective)* smartest *(related word: clever)*

confess *(verb)* to admit something *(related words: confessed, confessing)*

dawn *(noun)* the first light of morning

desperately *(adverb)* with a lot of need *(related word: desperate)*

dimmed *(verb)* became less bright *(related word: dim)*

dodging *(verb)* getting out of the way of something *(related word: dodge)*

expensive *(adjective)* costing a lot of money

humiliation *(noun)* embarrassment *(related word: humiliate)*

imaginary *(adjective)* made-up *(related word: imagine)*

innocently *(adverb)* not doing anything wrong *(related word: innocent)*

insults *(noun)* mean comments about someone

intensity *(noun)* strength

memorize *(verb)* to learn something by heart *(related word: memory)*

muscular *(adjective)* having a lot of muscles *(related word: muscle)*

nostril *(noun)* one of the two openings in your nose through which you breathe and smell

occasionally *(adverb)* once in a while

opportunity *(noun)* a chance

passport *(noun)* a booklet that says what country you're from. It is often necessary for travel.

permission *(noun)* the act of allowing something to happen

poetic *(adjective)* beautiful; said or done in a way that sounds like a poem *(related word: poetically)*

proposed *(verb)* asked someone to marry them *(related word: propose)*

reciting *(verb)* saying something that you have learned by heart

romance *(noun)* something having to do with love *(related words: romantic)*

scoundrel *(noun)* a bad person, especially one that cheats and lies

timid *(adjective)* shy

witty *(adjective)* funny in a smart way *(related words: wit)*